AF504447

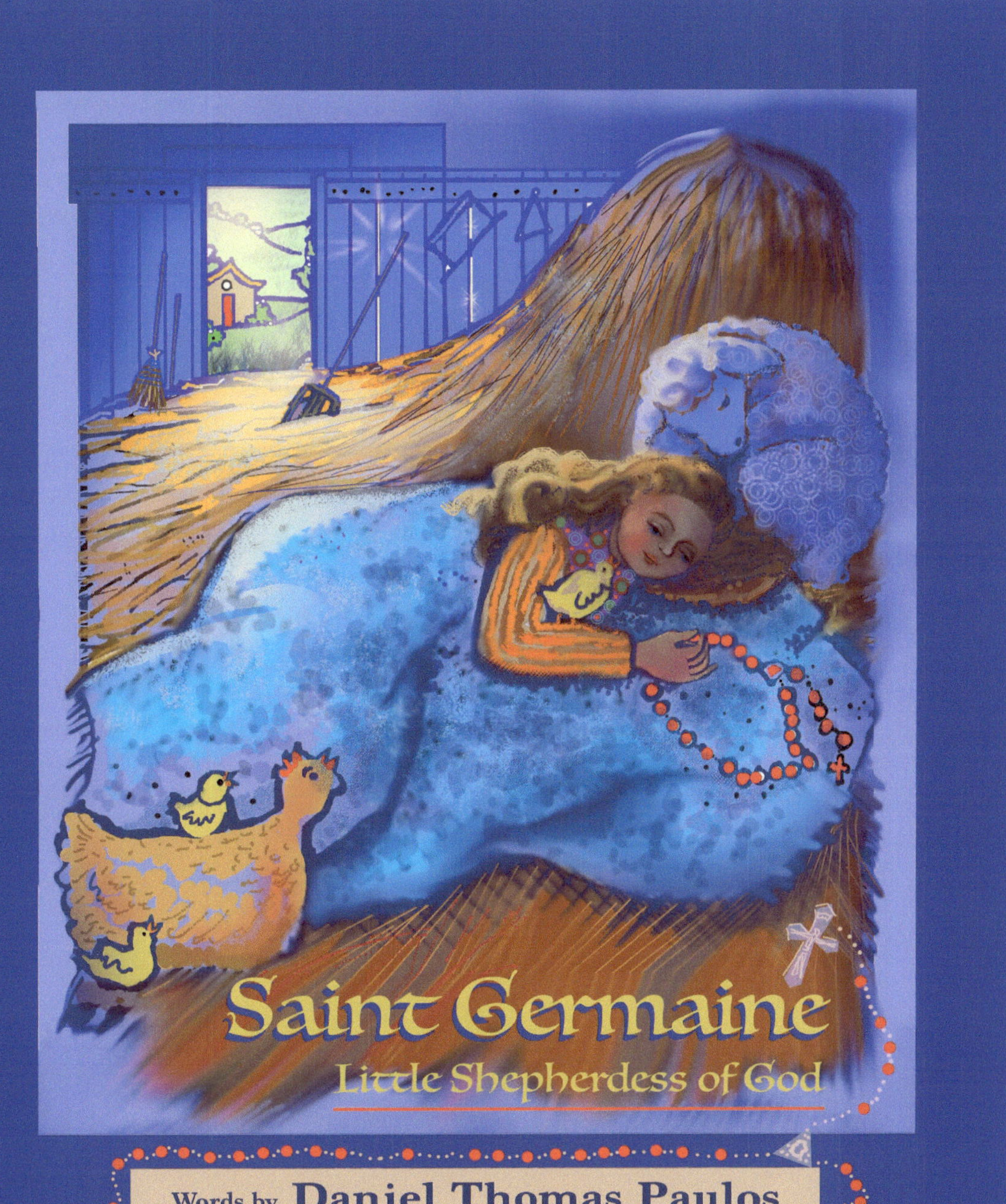

Saint Germaine
Little Shepherdess of God
Words by Daniel Thomas Paulos
Pictures by Anne Marie Simoneau

The waters were so happy to see her
That they parted as she crossed beyond

Published by
St. Bernadette Institute of Sacred Art
Post Office Box 8249
Albuquerque NM   87198-8249
United States of America

ISBN: 9798726106885

Saint Germaine
1579–1601

Many years ago a babe was born
With a crippled hand and arm
And soon after birth her Mama died
The family was robbed of its charm

They sadly worked and ate of the land
Surviving as best they could
Supporting a family without a mother
Caused emotions misunderstood

Known by all as Germaine Cousin
She was born at Pibrac in France
Before long her papa chose to re-marry
The stepmother gave her no chance

In fact, she was repulsed by Germaine
For she was ugly, deformed — but holy
No matter how kind Germaine was to her
The stepmother hated her solely

Turning father and siblings against her
Using her ailments to persuade
"If she doesn't stay away from this house
We'll all be afflicted" she bade

Forbidden to live with her family
Given scraps from the table
Though crumbs, she always shared
With the Poor near the stable

So Germaine had to seek refuge
She slept on hay in the barn
Animals warmed her on winter nights
And a blanket made of yarn

Germaine was alone much of the time
Leaving lots of space for praying
She learned to love the Lord Jesus
And to live what He was saying

When suffering pain or rejection
She often walked to the church
There she felt hugs from Jesus
She never had far to search

Once the town got to know her
Fear of contagion slipped by
No longer ugly, just "one of them"
Humbled, they made her cry

Germaine was placed in charge of the sheep
She served the flock with care
Daily, she led them to the grazing field
Fattened for the market square

Over the years her holiness grew
Her goodness was clearly known
Her father was scolded for abusing her
The seeds of contrition were sown

How could he treat his daughter like this?
Ashamed, he just wasn't thinking
He begged Germaine, "Please forgive me!"
She blushed, both eyes were blinking

"Oh no, Papa – no apology needed
The barn has become my home
Truly, I have everything a-plenty
I have no reason to roam"

Living alone for so many years
She loved walking to Mass
She'd poke her staff deep in the ground
Where her sheep knew not to pass

As if this marvel wasn't enough
She'd approach the glistening pond
The waters so happy to see her
Parted as she crossed beyond

One day as her stepmother watched
Germaine hid scraps in her apron
Knowing it was food, she ordered: "Stop!"
But then God humbled the matron

As the apron dropped the woman gasped
It wasn't bread but flowers
Germaine gave them to her guardian
Then ran from pouring showers

Germaine was never strong of stature
She was frail, quiet and free
Her father often watched her work
And waved, now fond was he

One day she didn't awaken for work
She had never failed her accord
So her father went to fetch her
She had gone Home to the Lord

Her father wept most bitterly
Her siblings sadly joined in
But not the wicked stepmother
Who smirked and glowed of sin

Germaine no longer had to hide
She's with Jesus in Paradise
No one there will call her ugly
And love alone will suffice

THE END

OTHER BOOKS BY DAN PAULOS

SPRING COMES TO THE HILL COUNTRY (Roman, Inc)

HE'S PUT THE WHOLE WORLD IN HER HANDS (Ignatius Press)

IN THE MIDST OF CHAOS, PEACE (Ignatius Press)

BEHOLD THE WOMEN (St. Bernadette Institute of Sacred Art)

A LIVING LOVE HURTS (Don Bosco Press, Tokyo)

DIO HA POSTO IL MONDO INTERO NELLE MANI MARIA (Vatican Library Press)

I, BERNADETTE (St. Bernadette Institute of Sacred Art)

REMEMBERING BERNADETTE (St. Bernadette Institute of Sacred Art)

Children's Books:

ELIZABETH – Princess of Heaven (St. Bernadette Institute of Sacred Art)

GERMAINE COUSIN—Little Shepherdess of God (St. Bernadette Institute of Sacred Art)

DOMINIC SAVIO (St. Bernadette Institute of Sacred Art)

THE STUPID ONE (St. Bernadette Institute of Sacred Art)

Music CDs Produced by Dan Paulos:

LOVING YOU (Songs of Miriam Therese Winter)

BREATH OF THE SPIRIT (Songs of Miriam Therese Winter)

A NEW DAY DAWNS (Songs of Miriam Therese Winter)

COME TO THE SPRINGS OF LIVING WATER (Songs of Miriam Therese Winter)

MACK BAILEY SINGS THE SONGS OF MIRIAM THERESE WINTER

Documentaries:

A SEEING HEART

MADONNA OF THE SLAUGHTERED JEWS

BERNADETTE (The story of the first pilgrim of Lourdes)

AMERICA'S SHRINE TO SAINT BERNADETTE